D1106269

FLORENCE FARR
BERNARD SHAW
W. B. YEATS

FLORENCE FARR
BERNARD SHAW
W. B. YEATS

Letters

Edited by CLIFFORD BAX

LONDON
HOME & VAN THAL LTD.
1946

PRINTED IN THE UNITED KINGDOM BY
J. W. ARROWSMITH LTD., QUAY STREET AND SMALL STREET, BRISTOL

PREFATORY NOTE

Mrs. W. B. Yeats and Mr. Bernard Shaw have, of course, given their permission for the letters in this book to be published. The reader, however, may be disposed to ask, as Mr. Shaw asked, " How the dickens did they come into your possession ? "

In 1912 I was living in an old Wiltshire manor-house. During the summer of that year my first wife (to whom, as " Mrs. Bishop ", Mr. Shaw refers in one of his letters) invited Florence Farr to stay with us. For me, still a very young man, this was a delightful event because, as a still younger man, I had heard Florence Farr speak some of Yeats's poems to the psaltery. At the time of our meeting she must have been about fifty, but she was still beautiful and no one who saw her could forget her starry eyes. She was, in fact, one of the four or five genuinely poetic women whom I have known. And during her stay with us we talked a good deal about occultism, one of her deepest interests, and it must have been on account of those talks that I came to possess the letters.

A little later, Miss Farr (she is the same person as " Mrs. Emery ") suddenly decided to leave England and to end her time in Ceylon. She entered a Vedantist seminary ; and I understood, subsequently, that she took the step because she knew that she had not long to live. Before she left England, Miss Farr, in the traditional manner of mysterious persons, sent me a locked Black Box, asking me not to open it until I should hear of her death. She died on April 29th, 1917, and when I saw that news, I opened the box. For me the result was

v

that I realised for the first time how humorous Yeats could be, and that I experienced a large increase of admiration for Mr. Shaw. He does not think much of his letters. I do, and posterity will.

We can see clearly in Mr. Shaw's letters that Florence Farr wanted success,—in the ordinary meaning of the word. They also show that she had too much personality to become a good actress. It seems, in fact, that she made the amateur's mistake of acting to herself and not to the audience. As an author she obtained about the same measure of recognition that she had already obtained as an actress.

She must have had some sense of humour, or Mr. Yeats would not have entertained her with amusing anecdotes : and she had her great moment as an actress when Mr. Shaw persuaded her to play Rebecca in Rosmersholm instead of Ellida in The Lady from the Sea. The whole London press, unaccustomed to Ibsen, and for once carried away by him, wrote of her performance as that of a new Rachel or Ristori. As a journalist, writing in The New Age, Miss Farr had another instant of limelight when she championed the cause of prostitutes and other unpopular persons ; and so, on the whole, we must admit that she made her little public mark, even if it was not deep enough to outlive her. Her many private friendships with clever men (on whom, by the way, she never became dependent) were unknown to her contemporaries ; but they will save her from being forgotten.

On this occasion, when I am associated with a book by the two most famous of these friends, I hesitate to suggest that many persons are more attractive if they have not qualified for the Dictionary of National Biography. Such renown is not always unfortunate in its effect. If Mr. Shaw were to be visited by a delegation of Moonmen, they would not be able to turn his head. It is too well screwed on.

I like to think how happy Miss Farr would be if she knew that these letters, which she kept so carefully, may now be savoured by many people ; and I am glad that, for some mysterious reason or unreason, she decided to give them to me and not, as we might have expected, to some friend of much longer standing. Reputations in literature are a perishable commodity ; but it is hard for me to imagine a time when the public should have no interest in Yeats and Shaw. Perhaps, too, this little book will preserve the memory of a woman who could inspire remarkable men.

CLIFFORD BAX

Inside the black box I found this note from Florence Farr :

July 28th 1912

I am off to Ceylon next month, and make this collection of letters : from G. B. Shaw, who has been a most faithful friend to me, although it was not until 1906 that he could tell me that he felt proud of me,—he also published " Jacklyn " for me in 1912 : from W. B. Yeats : from Robert Farquharson, or rather De la Condamine, who I always called my marionette : and from Sir Henry Colvile who worked in South Africa, and won and lost so much between 1900–1902.

AN EXPLANATORY WORD FROM Mr. SHAW

I made the acquaintance of Florence Farr in the eighteen eighties, when the Socialist revival of those years, in which I took an active part as one of the Fabian leaders and as an indefatigable platform orator, took me on many Sundays to the house of William Morris on the Mall in Hammersmith to lecture there in the converted coach house which served as a meeting hall for Morris's followers.

Florence was the daughter of Dr. William Farr, famous as a sanitary reformer in the mid-nineteenth century when he and Sir Edwin Chadwick were forcing us to realize that England was dying of dirt.

Florence had been born unexpectedly long after her mother had apparently ceased childbearing : she was possibly indulged as a welcome surprise on that account. Though Dr. Farr survived his wits and lost most of his means by senile speculations before his death in 1883, he left enough to enable Florence to live modestly without having to sell herself in any fashion, or do anything that was distasteful to her.

She went on the stage and married a clever actor who was a member of the well-known histrionic Emery family. There was some trouble (not domestic) that ended in his emigrating to America and passing out of Florence's life. She attached so little importance to the incident, being apparently quite content to forget him, that I had some difficulty in persuading her to divorce him for desertion by pointing out that as long as their marriage remained undissolved, he might turn up any moment with very serious legal claims on her.

Whatever the trouble was that took him out of the country Florence gave up the stage for the moment, and set herself to learn the art of embroidery under Morris's daughter May. She acted in an entertainment at the house on the Mall; and on this occasion I made her acquaintance, and had no difficulty in considerably improving it. She set no bounds to her relations with men whom she liked, and already had a sort of Leporello list of a dozen adventures, none of which, however, had led to anything serious. She was in violent reaction against Victorian morals, especially sexual and domestic morals; and when the impact of Ibsen was felt in this country, and I wrote somewhere that "home is the girl's prison and the woman's workhouse" I became *persona grata* with her; and for some years we saw a great deal of one-another, and I wrote the letters which follow. It was a one-sided correspondence; for I cannot remember that she ever wrote to me.

She played the heroine in my first play in 1892.* In 1894 the late Miss Horniman gave her money to produce modern plays at the old Avenue Theatre, now replaced by The Playhouse. The first production, inadequately cast and acted, failed; and Florence was about to replace it by my first play, when I wrote *Arms and the Man* for her instead, selecting the cast myself. With Yeats' *Land of Heart's Desire* as an exquisite curtain raiser it had a startling first night success, and kept the theatre open (average receipts £17) until Miss Horniman's money was exhausted.

Being bound to secrecy to avoid shocking Miss Horniman's Puritan family, Florence could not tell me who was backing her. Years later I had a dream in which I

* *Widower's Houses*, produced at the Royalty Theatre, December, 1892.

ix

went into a room and found Miss Horniman sitting there, whereupon I exclaimed "YOU were the backer at the Avenue". Next day I wrote to her and asked her whether this revelation had any foundation. The illusion to this in the letters suggests that she was displeased ; but that was only her way : she was one of those good women who do things, but are also incorrigibly cantankerous.

I made desperate efforts to work up Florence's technique and capacity for hard professional work to the point needed for serious stage work ; but her early life had been too easy. I failed, and had to give up worrying and discouraging her. She found the friend she really needed in Yeats. What she called "cantilating" for him was within her powers. We detached ourselves from one another naturally and painlessly ; and presently I got married.

I heard about her departure for the East, but had no suspicion that her health was impaired in any way until I heard that she had undergone an operation. I telegraphed urgently for full information. My anxiety pleased her ; and I learnt from her that the operation had been, so far, "successful". Months later, her sister wrote to me that she was dead.

G. B. S.

LETTERS FROM GEORGE BERNARD SHAW
TO FLORENCE FARR

In the train—1–5–91

I HAVE not time to write at all unless I can snatch a scrawl in this way whilst I am running about.

I also am fascinated by your proposal, oh my other self—no, not my other self, but my very self. Now is it all over and utterly dead, as if it had never been. We are mere acquaintances, my dear Mrs. Emery, just as we were that day at Merton. And so we are FREE— to begin it all over again. I am a beggar once more ; and once more I shall come into my great fortune. I am again an unscrupulous egotist with a remorseless will ; and again shall I be moralized and have my backbone sweetly stolen away. We shall even have Rosmersholm again—but that reminds me of another matter.

There is nothing that drives me to such utter despair as when I make some blundering and unsuccessful attempt to make you see some technical point that my mother can teach to any idiot in a few lessons ; and you shrink as if I were disparaging your artistic gifts. You do not know the importance of some of these tricks as regards health, economy of physical force, self-contained- ness and the like. If I break in on your artistic vein to urge them, it is because I have an extraordinary desire to make the most of you—to make effective and visible *all* your artistic potentialities—not seven eights or nine tenths, but all. And not, observe, merely as an actress, but as a woman. Your ability to act must only be a mere consequence of your ability to live. You are so real to me as a woman that I cannot think of acting being to you anything more than a technical accomplishment which I want to see carried to a high degree of perfection. For the born actress I have a certain contempt : for the woman who is a consummate artist I have a deep fellow-feeling. The one is a sham : the other a reality completely expressed. There is thus a certain sense in which I would have you despise acting as a " vocation ". It is the work that comes to your hand, and you must do it as well as it can be done ; but you must always be the mistress of your art and not the slave of its intoxications and excitements. In my own art I am ready, if only time be given me, to answer for the workmanship to the last comma ; and now, if " inspiration " comes, it does not half escape me : I know how to seize it and knead it so as to exhaust all the nutriment in it.

When Archer says you want grip, he misses the problem in your case. You will never proceed by way of grip, but by sustained beauty of touch. But touch on what ? On a conception of your part so complete that it accounts for every moment of Rebecca's time whilst she is on the stage. That is what demands such frightful labour of invention—such years of time. At present there are innumerable gaps and holes in your conception : it is whilst you are passing through these that your " grip " is lost. Yet these gaps with you are not absolute blanks. They are rather places where you fail in intensity of realization and certainty of execution. You fade rather than vanish. And at all times you yourself are there, never quite insignificant. I am always reassured when I see you : even when I am not satisfied, I am not disappointed : there is no air of failure in anything you do. And I am not impatient—only frightfully afraid that you will get impatient with me and my criticisms.

I saw Vezin at the Academy private view today, and he has not made up his mind about Rosmer. I urged him strongly to do it, though I foresee that he will be troublesome in certain ways, through not quite taking the part in. Still, he will have artistic qualities that will be invaluable to you.

I shall get to bed now without staying to discuss that other relation. At this moment I am in a contemptuous fury and vehemently assert that your Christmas estimate of it was the right one. Not for forty thousand such relations will I forego one forty thousandth part of my relation with you. Every grain of cement she shakes from it falls like a block of granite on her own flimsy castle in the air, the work of my own imagination. The silly triumph with which she takes, with the air of a conqueror, that which I have torn out of my own entrails for her, almost brings the lightning down upon her. Imagine being told—but I cannot write it. Damnation! triple damnation! You must give me back my peace.

If you are disengaged tomorrow afternoon, will you come to Prince's Hall (*not* St. James's, mind) on the enclosed ticket. The hart pants for cooling streams.

GBS.

247 Moorside Lane
Birmingham

My dear Mrs Williams

This is to certify that you are my best and dearest love, the regenerator of my heart, the holiest joy of my soul, my treasure, my salvation, my rest, my reward, my darling youngest child, my secret glimpse of heaven,

3

my angel of the Annunciation, not yet herself awake, but rousing me from a long sleep with the beat of her unconscious wings, and shining upon me with her beautiful eyes that are still blind.

Also to observe incidentally that Wednesday is the nearest evening that shews blank in my diary.

Yours truly
Joseph Mazzini Walker*

29 Fitzroy Square W.
4th May 1891

Miserable, ill-starred woman, what have you done ? When my need was at its highest, my weariness at its uttermost, my love at its holiest, I found darkness, emptiness, void. I cannot believe now that we shall ever meet again. Years have passed over me—long solemn years : I have fallen in with my boyhood's mistress, Solitude, and wandered aimlessly with her once more, drifting like the unsatisfied moon. Tears have dropped from my heart—tears of mortal disappointment, reminding me of the days when disappointment seemed my inevitable and constant lot. I have lost my faith in all the achievement and confidence since that time : whatever my dreams may have been, I have slept where I was born, in the valley of the shadow. How could you do this thing ? Are there no subtle fluids, no telepathic wires, to tell you when the chapter of accidents sets me free from my chains ? This was to have been the happiest of all my great happinesses, the deepest and restfullest of all my tranquillities, the very inmost of all my loves.

* This letter is undated, but from internal evidence it should obviously come early in the series.

And I was robbed of it in the moment of embracing it by your caprice, your wanton caprice—you told me you had nothing to do. And I contrived so ingeniously, so patiently ; sent my mother to the opera ; induced a colleague to break an engagement I was bound to keep with him ; left one meeting early and gave another the slip ; and for what ? Wretch ! selfish, indifferent, heartless wretch ! A million reproaches on you for ever and ever. Farewell : all the happiness I owe you is cancelled and the balance is now on the other side—a huge balance, incalculable, unliquidatable. You can never repay me.

GBS.

at H. S. Salt's
Oxted Surrey
20–8–91

I am at present grovelling among the thistles and bees on the brink of a sandpit. The rain was trying to dislodge me an hour ago, and now the sun is having a turn. Nothing could have been less successful with me than the country air. I am only just recovering from the misery into which I was plunged by a sleepless night in a bed about 5 ft 2 in long in the restless, demagnetized atmosphere of this pretentiously rural place. If I hold out until Saturday afternoon I shall have endured the utmost that nature can sustain.

Prithee persevere with the speaking : I found with unspeakable delight last time that you were beginning to do it quite beautifully. There is much more to be done, of course, much ill usage in store for you, but success is now certain. You have reached the stage of the Idiotically Beautiful. There remain the stages of the

5

Intelligently Beautiful and finally of the Powerfully Beautiful ; and until you have attained the last you will never be able to compel me to recognise the substance of that soul of which I was shown a brief image by Nature for her own purposes.

The heat grows insufferable : I must up and away. Yet last night the country was covered with icebergs.

GBS.

29 Fitzroy Square W.
28th January 1892

I spent last evening arranging old papers and thinking. Result :—when the thinking was over it was going on to three o'clock—time to go to bed. Otherwise I should have written.

Now listen to me, will-less girl. When you tell me that I best know what I am, I assent, not with humility, but with towering head striking against every star and raising great bumps on them ; so that astronomers reel amazed from their telescopes. Cubits high and fathoms deep am I the noblest creature you have yet met in this wood of monkeys where I found you straying. Some of them thought you a pretty female ape ; others thought you a goddess : the first asked you to play with them ; the second asked to be allowed to worship you : you could not say No to either. Then come I, the man, and make you my woman on your stopping me as I wandered lonely through the forest and asking me to look earnestly at you. For many years had I wandered alone, sufficient to myself : I will, at a word, wander on again alone. But what will you do ? return to the monkeys ? It is not possible : self-sufficient must you also become or else find no less a man than I to be your mate.

There are two sorts of genius in this world. One is produced by the breed throwing forward to the godlike man, exactly as it sometimes throws backward to the apelike. The other is the mere monster produced by an accidental excess of some faculty—musical, muscular, sexual even. A giant belongs properly to this category : he has a genius for altitude. Now the second order of genius requires no education : he (or she) does at once and without effort his feat, whatever it may be, and scoffs at laborious practice. The first order finds it far otherwise. It is immature at thirty, and though desperately in need of education (being less a child of Nature by so much more as it is advanced in evolution) can find nothing but misleading until it laboriously teaches itself. I am a genius of the first order ; and so are you ; but I know my order and the price I must pay for excellence, whereas you are always appealing to the experience of the second order to justify your own self-neglect.

You are wrong to scorn farcical comedy. It is by jingling the bell of a jester's cap that I, like Heine, have made people listen to me. All genuinely intellectual work is humorous. You can create your part in a farcical comedy : in Rosmersholm you can only offer yourself as an imitation of something created by Ibsen. I wish to see you an accomplished actress. When you get your part in the first piece, I insist on your reading it over to me. When you are a highly skilled hand, and all difficulties about engagements and money disappear, then we will consider further.

Now I must fly, only stopping to say that I challenge any analyst to find one base ingredient in my regard for you ; but I will not face the Judgment bar at the end of

7

my life with you if I am unable to meet the question, " Why did you suffer her to do her work badly ? "

your taskmaster

GBS.

29 Fitzroy Square W.
27th April 1893

The unspeakable absurdity of that performance is only surpassed by the unparalleled blastedness of the play. Even the two men in the gallery who had got their orders from Flemming, and who strove so heroically to make a reception for him, were paralysed as the play jingled its poor old wires along. Why do they not strike out all those painful allusions to the crowded state of the house and to the histrionic capacity of the people on the stage.

The last act is simply ridiculous. Irving in The Iron Chest gnawing the boards and saying " Whep me, ye grenning fiends " was modern and plausible in comparison. Janet* was transcendently bad. In the scene in the dark, and the recitation scene, I thought she was letting you get ahead out of pure consideration for me ; but the finale destroyed that romantic illusion. To her infinite credit, the more she tries to make the play live, the more ghastly and ridiculous become its antics. Charrington comes off best. The Abbé is like a jack-acting amateur. Saxe's coat and the Duchesse's gloves are badly in want of cleaning ; and you ought to powder your own hair and go about every day as an old woman whilst the piece lasts, the wig being only fit for a Salvation Army drum-stick.

* Janet Achurch. The play is " Adrienne Lecouvreur."

8

In the first scene you are insufferable. You wave your arms about like a fairy in a transformation scene, obviously *pretending* to make an impossible toilet. You must invent something real to do, or else simply put on the patch intently, carefully, resolutely (as becomes a poisoner-potential) and then study yourself thoughtfully in the glass, like an artist in the art of dress. If you decide at any time to do nothing, shut your mouth, and compose yourself, and *do* nothing. As a *grande dame* you should never be at a loss and never in a hurry. You should speak a little at least with your lips, and not say " supposcitisnotformebutforanother " so as to strike the house dumb with its utter want of any intention or meaning. As to the way you tighten your upper lip, and bunch up your back, and stiffen your neck, and hold on by your elbows, that is, I admit, necessary to prevent you falling forward on your nose, and it is good for the calves and lumbar muscles, which are developed by the strain. I sacrifice this advantage on the platform and in the street by balancing my torso on my pelvis, and my head on my torso, so that they stand erect by their own weight. This lazy practice would also enable me, by a very slight movement of my head, to draw back with some dignity from Saxe in the first act, at the flower incident.

In the passages of action you manage to make a sort of success. So could anybody, I conclude. In the recitation scene Janet gives away the scene by bad stage management. The old style—the Princess and the audience grouped R, and Adrienne beginning L in profile and crossing as she grows more vehement—was far better. You should not put the cap on openly by rising to receive the charge. You should insult Adrienne by not attending to her, turning your face to the audience, playing with your face as you feel that she is approaching you, but not

9

looking at her until she has finished the last line she hurls at you, when you should spring up and face her for the first time. Your rising earlier spoils her speech, which is already hampered by the small room and unimposing arrangement of the tableau. I wish I could get over tomorrow to go over the part with you, especially the first scene, which is very badly talked; but it's impossible. Friday and Saturday are jam full. On Sunday I have to lecture at Bow at half past seven.

The sooner the play disappears, the better for the reputation of the Charringtons and their enterprise. But you rather score off it; and I advise you to make the most of it while it lasts.

GBS.

(Letter-card)

29 Fitzroy Square W.
12th October 1896

Lost wretch. I have not yet recovered from the announcement that you are the true author of Ibsen's lifework. How can I or anybody or anything console you now? You would not believe in my doctrine of working at some reality every day; but you none the less worked every day at your unreality. And now you think to undo the work of all those years by a phrase and a shilling's work of exoteric Egyptology.*

As for me, I can wait no longer for you: onward must I go; for the evening approaches. To all your flower-maidens I have given more than you gave me, and

* "Miss Farr wrote a small book called "Esoteric Egyptology."

10

offered more than any of you would take. My road is the highroad ; and your bypaths and shortcuts only lead backward. I have often looked down them and sometimes laughed, sometimes warned you vainly. Now a great horror and weariness comes on me. I cannot help anyone except by taking help from them ; and you cannot help me. You have brains and imagination—the means of deceiving yourself, without faith, honor, heart, holiness—the means of saving yourself. I have the greatest regard for you ; but now to be with you is to be in hell : you make me frightfully unhappy. What *is* " the true relation " between us ? The relation of the North Pole to the South. Forgive me ; but you have driven me to utter desperation : I can no longer be satisfied to suffer and shake my fist at the stars.

GBS.

(Letter-card)

29 Fitzroy Square W.
13th Oct. 1896

You wretch—to write me a nasty letter just when a really sympathetic, original woman would have written a particularly nice one. After all these years, too, with the advantage of my precepts ! I am ashamed of you. I blush—I apologise to posterity for your conduct. You are incorrigible. Is it *my* fault ? Have I not tried and tried and tried, lectured, protested, warned, implored ? Do you want me *for ever*, greedy one ?

GBS.

29 Fitzroy Square W.
14*th Oct.* 1896.

Serve you right!

I hereby warn mankind to beware of women with large eyes, and crescent eyebrows, and a smile, and a love of miracles and moonshees. I warn them against all who like intellectual pastimes ; who prefer liberty happiness and irresponsibility to care, suffering and life ; who live for and in themselves instead of for and in the world ; who reject the deep universal material of human relationship and select only the luxuries of love, friendship, and amusing conversation.

I declare before creation that you are an idiot, and that there never has been, never can be, is not now, nor in any yet to be discovered fourth dimension of time ever shall be, so desperate and irreclaimable an idiot, or one whom Destiny has mocked with greater opportunities.

I renounce spiritual intercourse with you. I condemn you during all our future meetings and bicycle rides, to talk instead of listening. I may possibly, being the greater intelligence, learn something from you. From me you can learn nothing. Worse, you can mislearn.

GBS.

The Argoed. Penallt. Monmouth.
8th September 1897

It is frightful—appalling—how the time rushes by here. I have not drawn rein for a day ; and yet "You Never Can Tell" is not ready for the printer. It is the dullest trash I ever revised : " Widowers' Houses " is worth fifty such.

There is nothing mysterious or peculiar to yourself in the fact that you get work only when people want you and not when you want them. That is everybody's experience. But it is by the failures that you gain the power to pick up the windfalls. If you had learned the whole repertory of Sarah Bernhardt, Duse and Ellen Terry and practised them until you had been refused a chance of appearing in them by every manager in London, the failures of the Poisoned Garden and the Comedy of Sighs would have been personal successes for you, just as Marie Tempest achieved her position by appearing in a ghastly and ludicrous failure called " The Fay o' Fire " at the Opéra Comique. I never had anything accepted ; but if I had never written the five long novels and the bushel of articles that were refused I should not have been able to do the work that finally offered itself to me. If you change your name you will simply throw away the advantage of what you have done. Your belief in the miraculous is irrepressible. Probably I wont succeed in persuading you that there is no charm at work to be counteracted by some ceremony (changing your name and throwing a pinch of salt over your left shoulder come to the same thing) ; but I can only tell you again that you must keep on knocking your head against the stone wall until it gives way. Only, remember the saying " Knock, and it shall be opened unto you." There's no use in waiting if you dont " knock ", or in thinking that the knocking is no use because the door will certainly open somewhere quite out of earshot of the knocks. Besides, the chances are enormously against a haphazard offer hitting on a haphazard vacancy. If you offer your services as dramatic critic to the Saturday Review, they will decline simply because they have a critic already ; and the refusal is no more disparaging than your refusal of a coster's offer of a vegetable that you happen to have in the pantry. Wait for the usual fifteen years or so and you will fit yourself in somewhere.

I am alarmed to hear of your treatment of the 700 pounder. Why overdo things ?

The wind has changed to the east ; and " You Never Can Tell " has bored me to death. I am in the most disagreeable humor possible.

GBS.

10 Adelphi Terrace W. C.
13 *Dec.* 1900

There is no use arguing with Christy. Simply say, Have you tried ? He doesnt know the Ibsen streak in modern tropicalism : all you can say is that you know it's there and you want to find out what it's worth. If he wont try, then there is an end of the matter. There is no class of clients in the world that doesnt take an interest in the theatre. Tell him that you have baited your hook in the way that your experience suggests to you will prove attractive—that you are perfectly aware that it is out of the common groove—that you know no more than he does whether the people who found £6000 for you to run a London Theatre with are represented throughout the country by tens or hundreds of thousands—but that you want him to drop the hook into the water and see whether anybody will bite. If he will, let him drop it in forthwith and let you know the result. If he wont, let him say so and be damned.

14

Your request about the rehearsal is an innocent one. There are *no* rehearsals of " Captain Brassbound." The cast is very nearly complete ; and there will probably be some sort of performance on Sunday ; but we are not within a month of anything so regular as a full rehearsal. I will try to get you a ticket for Sunday though I am told that the members* have bespoken every seat in the house. If that is so I will get you a ticket for the matinée.

GBS.

10 Adelphi Terrace W. C.
6th June 1902

No : I should do no good by entering into cantilationary polemics. I was thinking of writing to you in a precautionary manner before your letter came. The fact is, there is no new art in the business at all : Yeats thinks so only because he does not go to church. Half the curates in the kingdom cantilate like mad all the time. Toastmasters cantilate. Public speakers who have nothing to say cantilate. And it is intolerable except in the one obvious and complete instance—the street cry. Sarah Bernhardt's abominable " golden voice ", which has always made me sick, is cantilation, or, to use the customary word, intoning. It is no use for Yeats to try to make a distinction : there is no distinction, no novelty, no nothing but nonsense.

However, you might get some teaching out of all this advertisement. The psaltery amuses people ; and there is no reason why they should not use a string or a pipe to

* Of the Stage Society.

15

D

remind them of the normal pitch of their voices. But for practical teaching the old rule remains : take care of the consonants and the vowels will take care of themselves. You want to get first an athletic articulation. With that you can give effect to the real thing, which is, your sense of the meaning of the words, your emotional and intellectual conviction. That is the only thing makes speech tolerable. Without it cantilation can do nothing except intensify ordinary twaddling into a nerve destroying crooning like the maunderings of an idiot-banshee. Remember that even in singing, it is an Irish defect to lose grip and interest by neglecting the words and thinking only of the music. Cats do the same thing when they are serenading one another ; but the genuineness of their emotion gives them poignancy.

Moral : keep your head ; and dont let your nieces cantilate or atalantilate* anything in public until they can first *say* the piece interestingly and articulate it delicately and penetratingly. I have never been able to knock enough articulation into you, though you are much better than you were. You still think of how you are doing your recitations instead of what you are saying. The final consonant withers, and the light of the meaning goes out every now and then as you attend to your psaltery instead of to your business. At which moments I feel moved to throw things at you. And Yeats is heaping fresh artificialities and irrelevances and distractions and impertinences on you instead of sternly nailing you to the simple point of conveying the meaning and feeling of the author.

In haste

GBS.

* Miss Farr used a chorus from Swinburne's " Atalanta in Calydon" in her psaltery-recitals.

10 Adelphi Terrace W. C.
11th June 1903

The lady has very sharp ears and is clever beyond her occupation ; so I thought it best to warn you that your conversations—which were likely to be many and intimate between the acts at the Stage Society—would not be private.

The impression derived by the other lady was one which every Irishman conveys to every lady; and in those remote days I had not quite realised the matter-of-factness of social intercourse in other countries. However, as I never had a private conversation with her in my life, and can hardly have met her half a dozen times, no harm was done.

Are you too busy psalterying to copyright my new play* at the Bayswater theatre ? It is frightfully long —the first and third acts alone are longer than Hamlet ; but cutting is permissible provided enough is performed to leave the unperformed parts useless to pirates.

GBS.

Strachur, Loch Fyne, Argyllshire
15th Sept. 1903

All I can say about these Rig-Vedas† is that those who advise you to throw them into narrative form are, as might be expected, dolts. They will interest nobody but the people who have taken up this particular craze ; and the dialogue form will be more convenient for them than a nonsensical attempt to adapt it to the Strand Magazine

* Probably " Man and Superman."

† The Rig-Vedas, those exceedingly ancient Indian religious hymns, had clearly fascinated the part of Miss Farr's mind which was perhaps the least congenial to Mr. Shaw and the most attractive to Mr. Yeats.

people who would have nothing to do with it on any terms. Do not be misled by sloppyminded lunatics ; if you want to write popular books, write them : if you want to write mystic gospels, write them ; but in the name of commonsense dont try to popularise your mysticism or to mystify your popular readers. If preachee, preachee : if floggee, floggee ; but no preachee floggee too.

(The rest torn off)

10 Adelphi Terrace W.C.
30 *June* 1904

I am off on Saturday to The Old House (my new house), Welwyn, Herts, to write a play ; and if I come up my afternoons will be engaged most likely : in fact it is only such engagements (Fabian Committees etc.) that will drag me from my work. I have spent a month in Rome and have done nothing but Election business and Candida rehearsal since February, the result being acute unhappiness at my wasted life. I will do nothing but write for the rest of the year.

Sweet* must tell you about the phonetics. He will probably say that two years residence at Oxford is indispensable, as he has a genius for making everything impossible both for himself and everybody else. He is the most savagely Oxonian and donnish animal that ever devoted his life to abusing all the other dons. His desk is full of MS novels devoted to the exposure of all the humbugs and sciolists and sham philologists who have obstructed him for the last twenty years. He is a satirist, a genius, all ideas, and all spite and parochial Oxford tittle-tattle. When I arrange for him to write a magazine article on the burning topic of Languages and the

* The late Henry Sweet, pre-eminent in Phonetics.

Empire, he sends the editor a libel on one of his professorial opponents which would cost the Review about £5000 in costs and damages, and would interest nobody. His worldly incompetence is beyond words ; and yet he is not a fool—quite the reverse. See him and try what you can make out of him.

My plan is simply that you should learn the science of pronunciation and become a professor of phonetics for dramatic purposes. I am sure that Tree* would put down a professor of phonetics on his list of teachers for the mere novelty and look of the thing, especially if you made it clear that you were not going to interfere with Rosina Filippi.

GBS.

Is the trip to Oxford and residence there for long enough to learn something a financial possibility ?

10 Adelphi Terrace W. C.
8th Feb. 1905

This Philanderer affair has knocked me endways. I thought it was an ordinary amateur business for a charity ; and now it turns out to be a sort of junior Stage Society. I must try to save the situation by barring any invitations to the press. Miss Murby, who has written about it, is a very clever young woman—a Fabian, who is firmly persuaded that my views on the production of the Superman involve the forcible coercion by the State of selected women to breed with selected men ; and she, being a good-looking and clever person, very likely to be selected under such a scheme, fears the worst. Now I protest that I never proposed anything

---

* Sir Herbert Tree had recently started his School of Acting.

more compulsory than offering, say £2000 for a satisfactory baby, *à prendre ou à laisser*, as the lady likes.

If you are going to stage-manage, so much the better. I will go down with you and start the affair—arrange the business etc, as I may as well learn this confounded play now. I go down to Leeds next Tuesday ; but except for that I shall be in town rehearsing " How He Lied " at the Court—fairly free in the evenings, I hope.

GBS.

The Old House,   10 Adelphi Terrace
  Harmer Green, Welwyn.   W. C.
    5th March 1905

Out of town, as you see. I am getting quite maddened by the business (mostly refusing it) that my recent boom has brought on me. It is enough to make one curse the day I ever wrote a play. If I would consent, the whole 13 plays would be produced simultaneously about the middle of April.

By the way, are you arranging the choruses for the Trojan Women* ? If so be very discreet about using modern fashionable discords. In the Hippolytus, towards the end, you began to ramble up and down staircases of minor thirds in a deplorable manner. I strenuously advise you not to introduce deliberate figuration of discords. The effect is modern, cheap and mechanical.

Stick to the common chord, major and minor, and avoid sequences and figurations. I should stick to the

* Professor Gilbert Murray's version of Euripides' tragedy.

old lines of Cherubini's counterpoint, which grew out of unaccompanied vocal harmony and barred not only discords, but even the six-four position of the common chord. ♯♯ The moment you begin to figure diminished sevenths and the like, Euripides gives way to Liszt, and the harmony becomes *instrumental* in its suggestion. In haste, haste, oh Lord !

GBS.

Derry, Rosscarbery, Co. Cork.
(until October)
31st July 1905

Dear Florence—one must call you something—I have the gravest doubts about Candida, and indeed about your project generally. Candida is well known in Germany through Agnes Sorma's playing ; and Salome has been played to death there since its great success a year or two ago. Of course this is so far favourable to an English company, because people like to see a play they know when they venture on a foreign language. But only a very strong company could sustain comparison between the German casts at the Deutsches Theater etc. and your own people. Candida is not in your line ; and to play it after the leading German actress in that line would not be the most prudent thing that you could do. Farquharson is very clever, and might do something with Eugene ; but Candida without a really powerful and brilliant Morell is a ghastly business. You are not likely to get a better company than the last Candida one at the Court ; and yet we have withdrawn the play there because it went to bits very much as Arms and the Man did after the first night.

Besides, these foreign experiments hardly ever pay, except as advertisements for further activity. Whose money is to be in it ? if yours, then NO. I will not be an accomplice in your ruin.

The Germans, unacquainted with Rossetti, Swinburne etc. etc., enormously overestimated the originality and value of Salome ; and it may be that Binyon and Symons would interest the Germans more than they interest our Philistines. But Binyon's Tristan has to stand against Wagner's, with which the Germans are saturated. Furthermore, these verse plays need just that sort of trained professionalism which we are weak in and the Germans relatively strong. Have you any other cantilagors available ?

A. Entsch, 7 Neue Wilhelmstrasse I, Berlin W. is the leading agent.

Let me know whether on sane consideration you still think the project feasible.

GBS.

10 Adelphi Terrace. W. C.
2nd December 1905

I thought it was the 15th Dec, worse luck !

I have never seen Miss H.* since the old days, and very much doubt whether I should recognize her if I met her now. But since the foundation of the Irish Literary Theatre, we have corresponded to the extent of two or three exchanges of letters in reply to her sending me a notice of performances etc. Her tone is generally that of a woman pursuing a quarrell (sic) with a person she violently dislikes ; and when I first suggested that I thought

* Miss Horniman, presumably.

22

the time had perhaps come for verifying my dream about the Avenue backer, she was furious. I gather from Yeats that he also was pulverized for hinting at such a possibility. But my recollection of her is not of an unamiable woman ; and I have always assumed that she was simply shy, frank, and original, a combination which generally leads, on conventional assumptions, to a terrifying impression. And I seem to be on the right track with her. So dont assume that she dislikes you merely because she expresses herself in her characteristic manner.

I think it likely that she was shy about the Avenue business because it seemed at the time a ridiculous failure. Now that she has successfully launched the I. L. T.,* and that she was the original discoverer and encourager of the great G. B. S. (a post for which there is immense competition nowadays—the claimants including all our leading managers) the matter wears a different complexion, and you may claim to have done very well for her—No more room.

GBS.

Mrs. P. C. is a clever and lovely child of about 13.† By all means tout with her.

Edstaston, Wem, Shropshire.
27th Dec. 1905.

I strongly deprecate the Cenci. It is out of date, false in sentiment, and ludicrously unreal to the sort of audience you want.

* The Independent Literary Theatre.

† We may assume that these words describe Mrs. Patrick Campbell.

E

As to the Superman scene, I do not say No ; and of course I dont want any fees (" where there is nothing the King loses his rights ") ; but have you realized the size of the job ? Is Ricketts taken with it ; for unless there is a really artistic fantastic picture, with top lighting in the manner of Craig, and cunning costumes—a violet velvet Don Juan (horribly expensive), a crimson scarlet Mephistopheles, a masterpiece of white marble sculpture, and a radiant female (will you radiate ?), the thing will be unendurable. And the stage must have a trap to work the change from the old woman to the young. And then, have you considered the appalling length of the parts ? Where will you find a Don Juan willing to learn that prodigious part, and intelligent enough to make it interesting. Think of the last act of " Barbara ", which is a trifle in comparison, and yet it almost drove the audience mad because Undershaft had not mastered his part sufficiently to make it interesting. You had better ask Barker ?—perhaps he will give you the Court Stage for it. The Superman is licensed ; and as *Judith** is not canonical but only apochryphal, there is no reason why Redford should not license it. The boxers' hall is not a very delightful place ; and the chairs are quite damnably uncomfortable ; nothing short of a glove fight could distract the sitters from their agony.

Of course Murray did not object to "Barbara." Was ever man so flattered ? He says it is extraordinary how very personal I can be without his seeming to mind, somehow.

I confess I think Monna Vanna a greatly overrated abortion. It seems to me as plain as a pikestaff that he had planned a really interesting play and that Georgette Leblanc insisted on his making it a " possible " one ; so that she might have a Sarah Bernhardt success. The

* " Judith," a one-act play by Sturge Moore.

24

first act is all right : one awaits with great interest the duel of sex in the condottiero's tent. It is clear that the lady is going to get out of the difficulty somehow, like Marina in Pericles or Lady Cicely in Brassbound : otherwise there will be no play. But when nothing more ingenious comes than " Dont you remember little Tommy ? " " Bless me ! It's little Liza ! My ! Only fancy ! ", a defrauded public is entitled to its money back ; and the business with the cloak becomes a mere indecency to get a vulgar laugh every time she pretends she is going to open it.

I dont see why you should not reblossom and have a great period now that you are about forty (I'm 50 !). In the old days you caught on prematurely to old men and egotists—Ibsen, a grim old rascal, Todhunter, exactly like God in an illustrated family Bible, and me, an unintentional blighter of every purpose but my own. You were eaten up and preyed on : now you can have your turn with the knife and fork whilst we, whitehaired and doddering, look on at you with watering mouths.

I return to town tomorrow for a few rehearsals to get Barbara straight for the evening bill on the 1st. I return here on the 4th. as a centre for electioneering in the north for about a week.

GBS.

Harmer Green
Welwyn.
4th April 1906

Suderman's Johannisfeuer has nothing to do with Herodias. It is a modern play in a farmhouse on St. John's Eve. Margaret Halstan is cast for the most Suderific part.

You will have to rehearse with some knowledgable person in front if you wish the new society to be a success. S. M's* play was full of absurdities (Archer quoted several of them); and the business did not fit into the lines. Ricketts' part of the business I thought good. There was the making of something in your Phaedra; but you really havnt (sic) any adequate idea of the work and the unrelaxing grip such a part demands. A great deal of it was inaudible, simply because you acted it to yourself confidentially without the slightest regard to the necessity for never letting go your grip of the man in the back row of the gallery. You did good bits, and then let the thing fall through until you felt interested enough to have another turn. It does not do to take care of the pounds and leave the pence to take care of themselves : they simply *dont*. Your standard of work—of mere physical exertion, I mean—is far too low. You want somebody with a whip to keep you up to the collar. Mrs. Bishop beats you hollow in this way : she is always doing her full share of pulling the dead weight of the play along, and getting in her acting on top of that. But you sugar disgracefully except where you see your way to an effect. It is perfectly maddening to hear you get hold of your part for a line or two, and then coolly drop it and let all the steam off. Murray asks whether you have not a mother with a large stick to keep you awake. Barker gives you up in tragi-comic despair, and declares that you positively *like* doing things feebly. In a way he is right ; for you have an idea that because the first hundred pounds of steam are not acting, but simply mere brute grip of the audience, they are inartistic. So they are ; but they are necessary, and should be automatic with all experienced public

* Presumably Mr. Sturge Moore.

performers. With your voice and looks and intelligence you would seldom be out of an engagement if only you would work as Wynne Matheson works. She would put as much nervous force into saying " My lord : the carriage waits ", as you would into " Give *me* the daggers." You take things so amiably easy that even your gestures becomes childish : you crisp your fingers from the knuckles when you should swing your whole arm from the shoulder, and your voice becomes easy and off hand and reassuring when the wretched author and manager want the audience to hear the tocsin in it.

But what's the use of talking. You dont believe me. All the same, *do* get somebody to produce the plays who will tell you when the scenes tumble to pieces.

GBS.

10 Adelphi Terrace W. C.
19th April 1904

Dear Madam (if that is not too familiar)

I am not the Stage Society : I am only an old buffer known to that highly respectable and up-to-date body as a relic of a bygone phase of affectation marked by Yellow Books, Keynotes novels, Beardsley, John Lane and other dusty relics of the day before yesterday. Doubtless I enjoy a certain consideration with them as a veteran celebrity ; but my connection with past ventures like the Independent Theatre etc. etc., is much against me, as the S. S. regards itself as the cultured and sagacious success that rescued the movement from all these disreputable failures. My wife is on the committee ; but she is one of the most convinced exponents of the above point of view except that she regards me as the greatest of all dramatists past or present, and is therefore specially down on all the previous enterprises which were so unworthy of my greatness. Such is the bias which people have towards their own property.

As to the acting, that doesnt matter—though I think they probably rather exaggerate your powers than under-rate them. But if you were Rachel, Ristori and Duse all in one, it would not be good business to act in the D. F.* if the S. S. performed it, because the S. S. can now get fairly fashionable casts ; and it is much more important to you to be played by fashionable actors and actresses than to act yourself. You had better send the play to the secretary Norman McKinnel, the Stage Society, Trafalgar Buildings, Northumberland Av. W. C., quite formally. It will get plenty of attention and excite some special curiosity. The danger is that it may be out of fashion ; but the S. S. has a remarkable power of being behind the time : most of them are only just coming in sight of where you were ten years ago. Mc Kinnel will send it to Everard Fielding, now acting as chief librarian (vice St. John Hankin, abroad), and he will send it round to the rest, including Charlotte, who is not (all things considered) a hostile witness.

I shall harp a little on my old notion that you should go down to Oxford and study phonetics with Sweet (York Powell could tell you about him). Someday I shall put in very strongly for the need of really scientific phonetic training for actors, and denounce all this Dramatic School stuff as nothing but Ryder all over again. If you were really to fill the opening you might —if Tree's experiment developed into anything perma-nent—make an original and solid and lasting place for yourself as a teacher.   GBS.

* Probably a dramatic version of Miss Farr's story " The Dancing Faun."

Hafody Bryn, Llanbedr,
Merionethshire. R. S. O.
(until September 30th)   7th Sept. 1907

No : dash me if I will. You must get Murray or
Orage* if you want a lecture on Dionysus. Do you suppose I have no more sense of the dignity of my sex, that
you would make me a curtain-raiser for a beauty show ?
I know too well the sort of figure a man cuts on such
occasions. I have just been the victim of a Man Hunt
on the Welsh mountains ; but the protagonist of a
Woman Hunt I will not be on any terms.

                                                    GBS.

                            (Postcard)

                            10 Adelphi Terrace W. C.
                                    23rd Nov. 1907

The run on Waste† is enormous : I dont know whether
it will be possible to get a seat for Tuesday, as the whole
European press has to be accomodated in addition to our
Sabbatarian members. If I can snatch one I will.

                                                    GBS.

                            The Bell Hotel
                            Gloucester.
                            14th Aug. 1909

I am on my way to the west of Ireland via Fishguard.
My address will be The Southern Hotel, Parknasilla,
Sneem, Co. Kerry.

* The late A. R. Orage, editor of " The New Age."
† " Waste " : a play by Granville-Barker, produced by the Stage
Society.

What on earth do you mean by your reading sight ? Everybody's reading sight goes after 40 : I have not been able to read without spectacles for many years. Is it more serious than that ? If it is, how could you do any work that could not be dictated to a typist ?

The National Theatre is now in the hands of a paid organizer who provides his own staff ; so I can do nothing there.

Why depend on agents ? They are no use, except to very incapable or very busy people who deal in short and frequent bits of work.

Send me a line to say what is really the matter with your eyes. I shall reach Parknasilla about Thursday. I am motoring.

GBS.

9.45.

I started early this afternoon to have a glorious ride with you from 4 to midnight. The glory, unfortunately, got concentrated into a much shorter period. After lunch, as I was coming to the foot of the Haymarket after passing the National Gallery, a railway van came out of the Haymarket and made for Cockspur St. Suddenly the horse shied and plunged up towards the Nat. Gallery on his wrong side. I was going pretty fast and I hit him with the nicest accuracy in the middle of the breastbone. I went down in a forest of horse's legs, van wheels and whirling bicycle machinery ; but with a nimbleness surprising in one of my years I made a twist, a roll, a bound and a spring all in one. As I did it, crack, smash, split, snap went all the bones of the bike, and as I shot on my feet the tail of the van rushed past me, and from underneath it came an amazing iron spider with twisted legs and umbrella-blown-inside-out wings which had once been my bike. Then crowd, police, frantic enquiries, names and addresses exchanged, driver of van too unspeakably relieved at finding that the smashed thing under his van was not me to deny that he was in the wrong : finally a certain indignation at my heartless composure. The van took the ruins of the bike away ; and I walked off—to realise, presently, that my right knee and leg, on which I had come down, was beginning to stiffen. So I drove to Charrington's (having reasons for avoiding Fitzroy Sq.) and was stuped and nursed by Janet and treated as a bad accident case until about an hour ago, when I took a cab and found that you had given me up and gone off to Powell's.

I shall wait while I write a letter to the Great Western inviting them to make good the ruin wrought by their horse. I am a little shaken, I suppose, but not so much as by the smash last year in Wales. If I rest my leg I shall, I hope, be all right in time for Bayreuth.

Sorry to have wasted your afternoon ; but I did not realise that I was going to keep you waiting so long— I thought half an hour would be sufficient for surgical operations at Charrington's. The sooner I am in bed the better.

My trip to Brittany is off, I believe. We (the Webbs and I) will probably go to the east coast.

GBS.

A FOREWORD TO THE LETTERS OF
W. B. YEATS

I DO not know when Florence Farr and WBY first met,
but he first saw her as an actress during rehearsals of
Dr. Todhunter's *Sicilian Idyll*. He wrote, in his monthly
letter to *The Boston Pilot*, on May 17th 1890 : " I have
never heard verse better spoken than by the lady who
takes the part of the shepherdess heroine, Amaryllis."
The play was produced in " the little club theatre here,
in the red-bricked and red-tiled suburb of Bedford Park
where so many of we writing people live." He had
always ' sung ' his own verse—his father, John Butler
Yeats, writing six years earlier of " this youth of
eighteen " in a letter to Edward Dowden, says, " his bad
metres arise very much from his composing in a loud
voice, manipulating of course the quantities to his own
taste,"—and now Florence Farr's voice and striking
beauty (" she is an almost perfect poetic actress ")
seemed to make possible the modern poetic drama he had
begun to plan and write before he was seventeen. He
wrote for Florence Farr *The Land of Heart's Desire*, and
in 1899 she came to Dublin to play ' Aleel ' in the first
production of *The Countess Cathleen*. Five years later
he gave her *The Shadowy Waters* to play privately at a
London Theosophical Convention that he " might dis-
cover how to set it aright as a play."

The letters continually reveal how great an influence
she had on the shaping and re-writing of the early plays,
but they do not, I think, suggest the intimate friendship
of those many years. WBY once said to me " She was
the only person to whom I could tell *everything*." He

33

thought her career as an actress had given her a solitary,
perhaps unhappy, personal life and quoted a phrase of
hers, " When a man begins to make love to me I instantly
see it as a stage performance." Their brief love affair
came to an end because " she got bored." Later they
disagreed over some detail in the production of the re-
written *Shadowy Waters* and he took the play away from
her. He became absorbed in Abbey Theatre controver-
sies, perhaps she wrote to him that they bored her for he
writes " I will never mention it again." The correspondence however continued until her death in 1917 but the
only letters of hers that seem to have been preserved are
those written during her last years in India. Instead of
speaking to a Psaltery she is experimenting with a Vina,
" the image of man's subtle body," she is translating
Tamil poetry, she is " in the thick of politics and having
a really interesting life at last." She is plunged into an
active, concrete life ; " Fate has made all the important
people here ill . . . I am left with a power of attorney
. . . beside my own school supervision " (she was the
' Lady Superintendent ' of The Ramanathan College in
Jaffna which was opened in 1913) " I lay out a garden of
25 acres, the children that have fever, the children who
steal, the children who are so naughty no one else can
manage them are brought to me, I hear evidence and give
decisions. It is exactly like being Queen Elizabeth."
" You tell me that you are writing your memoirs and ask
if I would prefer to appear as myself or under another
name. Certainly I think it would be safer for me to be
known as myself ; my experience of being the ' green
lady ' in Moore's book was not exhilarating." In January
1917 she had an operation and writes in pencil " When
I found a report was being spread that I had a *boil*, I
was most indignant at being supposed to have such a

34

nasty disease. Cancer seems decent and dry. It is quite an experience for me as I have never been helpless in my life since I was a baby." She is gay and courageous about it all. Did she remember, I wonder, that she had written two years earlier to WBY on hearing from him that Mabel Beardsley was dying of cancer, " I am always glad to hear of someone making a brave end. I came here to make mine brave and I seem to have started another incarnation."

George Yeats.

NOTE

The punctuation and spelling in the original letters has been kept throughout.

LETTERS FROM W. B. YEATS TO
FLORENCE FARR

Fountain Court,
The Temple.

MY dear S S D D.* has the magical armageddon begun at last ? I notice that the " Freemans Journal " the only Irish paper I have seen has an article from its London correspondent announcing inevitable war and backing it up with excellent argument from the character of Cleveland. The war would fulfil the prophets and especially a prophetic vision I had long ago with the Mathers's, and so far be for the glory of God but what a dusk of the nations it would be ? for surely it would drag in half the world. What have your divinations said or have they said anything ? When will you be in town next ? Could you come and see me on Monday and have tea and perhaps divine for armageddon ?

Your ever
W. B. Yeats.

* Mrs. Emery and W. B. Y. belonged to a Secret Society (called the O. G. D.) for the study of occultism. The reference to Cleveland suggests the Venezuelan Crisis and Cleveland's message to Congress on December 17th 1895. Mrs. Yeats has, moreover, traced an article on the subject in the " Freeman's Journal " of December 19th 1895. This letter was therefore written, we may presume, in December of that year.

My dear Mrs. Emery,

I hope that your illness is no worse than a day's dis-comfort and that you will be able to come after all to-morrow. Of course if you are ill there is no more to be said, but if you can come it will be of importance for it is much more important for that lecture to go well than for the Irish Literary Society evening to go well. I shall be quite content if you do one single poem to-morrow. I have had a letter from the editor of the "Daily News" asking permission to interview me on the Theatre and the New Art. Now to-morrow's lecture is got up by people connected with the "Speaker" and the "Daily News." If the lecture goes well it will help towards other lectures. I have an invitation for instance, from Edinburgh and if only we can get a little credit for this double performance of ours it may enable me to get the Edinburgh people to invite us both. In some ways the Theatre is a more taking subject than the New Art itself. I have much more to say about it and can group all our activities under this one title. A rich subject like this will enable me to tax you much less. You will always be able to speak to the Psaltery much or little as

(unfinished)

at Coole Park,
Gort,
Co. Galway.
July 15

My dear Mrs Emery : I meant to write yesterday, for I have been afraid that I did not seem sympathetic enough about your accident. I had hoped to have some talk with you on Monday evening, or to get out to you on Tuesday and so learn how you were, but both became impossible. Please write and tell me for it must have been a great shock and I have been afraid that you may have been more shaken than you thought. I brought the book of Johnsons poems with me that I might send it you. Shall I send it while you are away from home or wait till you get there again? One of the covers has got a little soiled, on the journey as I think, but I shall get a vellum cover put on it when I get to London again? I am at work on *Shadowy Waters* changing it greatly, getting rid of needless symbols, making the people answer each other, and making the ground work simple and intelligible. I find I am enriching the poetry and the character of Forgael greatly in the process. I shall make it as strong a play as *The King's Threshold* and perhaps put it in rehearsal in Dublin again. I am surprized at the badness of a great deal of it in its present form. The performance has enabled me to see the play with a fresh eye. It has been like looking at a picture reversed as in a looking glass. When you went, Maclaggan, after another thrust at Narcissus (who " spoke the lines about holding a woman in his arms as if he were murmuring of his experiences in Piccadilly,") said " it was worth having the play done, well worth while, because Mrs. Emery was a delight. It was a great joy to hear her." Or some such words, even stronger words I think, which I cannot remember. There is a good notice of the play—very well written—in ' To-day ' where Synge and myself and Shaw are enumerated with Ibsen and Maeterlinck as great dramatists, you are commended for " fine imaginative power," and after you, Jules Shaw is praised with evident enthusiasm for his Aibric. Lady Cromartie was I think

39

really delighted with the Psaltery and when she comes here, which she does in August, I shall find if she could arrange for the Duchess of Sutherland to hear you.

Yours ever

(Signature torn off)

at Coole Park
Gort
Co. Galway
Friday Night.

My dear Mrs. Emery: I was about to write to you to-day, when I was sent off to catch perch for some catholics who are to dine here to-night—a fast day. Isn't that a medieval way of getting a meal ? I stayed out till I had caught six fish, enough for a dinner—and now the mail has gone. I am very sorry about your hurts—I am afraid you must have suffered a great deal and I think it was heroic of you to play the Psaltery that night. I am making a new play of ' the Shadowy Waters.' It is strong simple drama now, and has actually more poetical passages. Aibric is jealous of Forgaels absorbtion in their dream at the outset and ends by being jealous of Dectora. Instead of the sailors coming back drunk at the end Aibric comes to appeal to Forgael to go back to his own land but on finding that he is taken up with Dectora bursts out in jealousy. Forgael bids Dectora chose whether she will go back to his own land or not and she chooses to go on with him—then Aibric cuts the rope and leaves them. This gives me a strong scene at the end. I wish you could get a good verse speaker who is a man. I wish I could persuade you that you are mistaken over Fargusson.* I have been taken in in the

* Presumably, Robert Farquaharson, a close friend of Mrs. Emery.

same way more than once myself. When a young man has even a slight vulgar element—and it is not slight in Farguson—one thinks it will leave him as he grows older. I thought that about Le Galleon*—who had what seemed like genius. It never leaves them, but when the enthusiasm of youth is over it gets much stronger till finally all else has left them. I have never known an exception. Apart from all else Farguson is a man who always requires to be explained. Mrs. Shakespeare for instance thought his manner was personally very offensive to you off the stage. He is really impossible as an artist. I had to use the greatest self control over myself all through those rehearsals. Only my fear of making things difficult for you kept me quiet.

I want you to try and get me Paget's model for the *Shadowy Waters* scene. I will probably work out a scene for Dublin, which could be used by you if necessary. Our stage is nearly as big as the Court. I can probably get that harp under tow—we have carpenters and so one of our own now. We are in all likelihood to have a large scene dock next door this winter and will be able to work things out very perfectly. You must come over some time and see our scenery, when the show comes off. You will I think prefer it to Craig. It is more noble and simple.

Saturday.

I have an idea for a bicycle trip when I get back. I have my imagination fired by Chaucer and would like to hire a bicycle and go the journey of the Canterbury pilgrims from Southwark and Greenwich to Canterbury through Rochester. I do not see why we should not go with some harmless person to keep up appearances.

* Richard le Gallienne.

Tell me if you try *Saul* and if you try *The Daughters of Jerusalem*. I doubt of the long graver poems like *Dark Angel* having enough internal movement for the Psaltery. One wants changes of voice—even different speakers at times—and choral bits for singing. The danger of the Psaltery is monotony. A thing the antients were more alive to in all arts than we are—Chaucer for instance follows his simple, *Knight's Tale* with an unspeakable tale told by a drunken miller. If Morris had done the like—everyone would have read his *Earthly Paradise* for ever. By the by Chaucer in that same unspeakable tale calls a certain young wife 'white and small as a weasel.' Does it not bring the physical type clearly to the minds-eye? I think one wants that sort of vivid irresistible phrase in all verse to be spoken aloud—it rests the imagination as upon the green ground.

I have had a cold for some days and that is why my writing is so bad and my spelling.

Yours ever
W. B. Yeats.

Write soon. Lady Cormartie and Lady Margaret Sackville arrive next week. I will find out what can be done for the Psaltery.

at Coole Park,
Gort,
Co. Galway.
Wednesday.

My dear Mrs Emery: I am glad you are so much better—you spoke to the Psaltery very well but I was afraid—not because you did not hide it—that you were worse than you pretended to me. I am changing *The Shadowy Waters* on almost every page and hope you will be able to play the new version—I think if you investigated however you would find that ' the beautiful poetry ' was whenever you spoke and ' the irrelevant drama ' whenever Farquisson did. I am making Forgaels part perfectly clear and straightforward. The play is now upon one single idea—which is in these new lines—

> " When the world ends
> The mind is made unchanging for it finds
> Miracle, ecstasy, the impossible joy
> The flagstone under all, the fire of fires,
> The root of the world."

There are no symbols except Aengus and Aedaus and the birds—and I have into the bargain heightened all the moments of dramatic crisis—sharpening every knife edge. The play as it was, came into existence after years of strained emotion, of living upon tip-toe, and is only right in its highest moments—the logic and circumstances are all wrong. I am going to make some fine sharp verses for Forgael when he enchants Dectora and I have done a bit where he sees her shadow and finds that she is mortal. I have got into my routine here—always my place of industry. After breakfast Chaucer—garden for 20 minutes—then work from 11 till 2 then lunch then I fish from 3 till 5, then I read and then work again at lighter tasks till dinner—after dinner walk. To this I have added sandow exercises twice daily. Today I break the routine sufficiently to bicycle over to Edward Martyn's and dine there—I have therefore given up my fishing hour to writing. Mrs Ladenburg—the American who heard you on Monday week—recited some of Brownings *Saul* after you left to show it would do for you. She thinks you should try it. You might do it something like the Homer. It would be a change with the resounding masculine music.

I have sent you the Johnson.

Yours always
W. B. Yeats.

Coole Park,
Gort
Co. Galway.

My dear Florence Emery : Get the harp mended and I will pay the amount. I shall leave the harp with you for the present at any rate but I may want it in Dublin some time. If on the other hand you would prefer to have it altogether then do as you suggest—I will give it you with pleasure—but I think you had better let it be mine and have the use of it. I have dreamed of you several times lately. Last night you had a friend who, as you phraised it " meddled a little with crime." His name was ' Jehovah Cutthroat.' I distinctly remember being jealous and thinking it just like you. Lady Cromarty and Lady Margaret Sackville are here, and this has made life much more human as it means various entertainments. It leaves me little time after my work is over but *Shadowy Waters* is getting gradually finished —doubled in beauty. Lady Cromartie is as simple as a child and as innocent. She remembers a past life and her present is utterly over-shadowed by it. She remembers people so beautiful looking that the people now seem ugly and trivial. This past is intensely vivid and has appeared to her since she was a child—long before she knew of incarnations. She was at Tara and describes

44

curious details of that old life. She is less clever but has more nature than Lady Margaret. There has been a tea party, that the county may have a glimpse of these birds of paradize, and I am tired out after two hours strained conversation. One lady, who is boycotted so that nobody is allowed to work in her garden but the village idiot, was my share of the festival. She had a little intelligence, the others were as dull and as healthy as cabajes. I have been waiting to answer your letters until I could send you a long passage out of *Shadowy Waters*—the first meeting of Forgael and Dectora, but Lady Gregory is too tired with entertaining for me to dictate it for the present. Write again soon.

Yours ever
W. B. Yeats.

I think the Paris affair is going all right but it goes very slowly.*

* The headquarters of the " Secret Society " were in Paris. The reference may be, however, to Miss Maud Gonne.

Coole Park,
Gort
Co. Galway.
Sunday Sept. 30.

My dear Florence Emery : as a correspondent you are prompt but meagre—your last was anyway—four lines I think. I have been meaning to reply these two weeks past, but have been absorbed in *Deirdre*. What I wanted to do was to suggest your sending circulars and lectures to ' Hon. Sec, Philosophical and Literary Society Cork.' I was also going to give you the name of the sec, of an

45

Aberdeen society which has written me but on looking up his letters I find he has written from a French hotel and that I have neither the name of the society or the address. I shall have to find out these from a professor I know in Aberdeen. I have had a bad time with Miss Horniman, whose moon is always in the full of late, but hope a letter yesterday has quieted her. Miss Darragh* is trying to play her for the chances it may lead to : but Fay is doing quite the reverse for he has just encountered an enemy and they have fought with fists and with a result about which each is confused for each seems to mix up what he did with what he had hoped to do. In other words each claims that he has licked the other and Fays enemy says he will attack him next time ' before the public on the stage.' Fay meanwhile writes that the enemy ' will be sorry before he (Fay) has done with him.' I think after careful investigation that Fay had slightly the better for he was dragged off while imploring to be let finish. It is all about a young woman. Do not talk about it just now as I don't want it to get round to Miss Horniman's ears that people know about it. I have not time to interfere but I think, for certain reasons, they will have to fight it out. No signs of my book yet and only an advance copy of my *Spenser* but you will have both in good time. Miss Tobin is back in London—she is a charming talker—gave the Synge and the principal players a dinner and was delightful—but well if I should cross to London in the next month it would not be for her sake. I am getting restless—as the swallows do at this time of the year—but *Deirdre* has me tied to the

* A prominent actress of the time. No one ever referred to her except as " Miss Darragh," but Mr. John Parker (editor of " The Theatre Who's Who ") tells me that her first name was Gethyn. She died in December, 1917.

46

table leg. I enclose some lines I wrote this morning. They are Deirdre's words spoken to the Musician in expectation of death.

I have just been sent an absurd book—very expensively got up—called Osric and largely an account in bad verse of Oscar Wilde. At the end are several poems by the author in his own person—one to Robert Ross, very emotional and one to a negro boy whose 'lips like cupid's bow' are celebrated. There is an illustration of the author with a benign smile pointing at the negro boy, who is quite hideous, and looking much like a young missionary with his first convert.

Yours ever

W. B. Yeats.

(enclosure)

DEIRDRE

There's nothing here for tears—a king and queen
Who've been true lovers are about to die.
And what is that ? What is't but putting off
What all true lovers have cried out upon—
The too soon wearying body, barriers
That are not broken when lip touches lip,
And all those changes that the moon stirs up,
Or some worse star, for parting lip from lip
A whole day long. I'd have you laugh with me.
I am no more afraid of losing love
Through growing old, for temporal change is finished
And what I have I keep from this day out.

H

My dear Friend : It is a long time since I have heard
from you. Isn't the debt on your side—I think I sent
you my book—I am a little anxious (I have become so
since so long has passed without my hearing). You
spoke of being ' seriously ' out of sorts and then of being
all right ' in a week.' I assume that it was only a
passing upset. Do write and tell me how you are. I
have been overwhelmingly busy and thoroughly over-
worked. The theatre is now a success, if it goes on as it
is now we are through all our troubles. Last night for
instance was a revival of *Doctor in Spite of Himself*,
Hyacinth Halvey, *Riders to the Sea* and the house was full.
People standing up both in gallery and pit. The audience
have been steadily going up and this is the best yet. At
this rate with our present expenditure we are making a
profit—but of course we must raise salaries.

Since I wrote the above sentence Fay and Mrs. Fay
(they eloped and got married a week ago) have been in
and Fay ' I have come round to crow.' Both Lady
Gregory and I have been building castles in the air with
you for one of their inhabitants. We mean to get you
over to play for us presently. Miss Darragh is I notice
not popular with the company. She says such things as
' Why do you not get that caster screwed on to the table
leg,' instead of making enquiries and finding out that
that caster cannot be screwed on because the woman
who washes the floors and the stage carpenter have
quarrelled about it—and the stage carpenter would
sooner die than screw it on. She is considered to lack
taste in the finer feelings—at any rate she has got them

48

into the right state to welcome you. I think she will be very useful to us in a number of parts, but there are a number of others that neither she or our own people can touch. I do believe I have made a great play out of Deirdre—' the authors are in eternity ' etc.—most powerful and even sensational. I will get a copy made and send it you I think, as it may be some time before it is printed. The first musician was written for you—I always saw your face as I wrote very curiously your face even more than your voice and built the character out of that. I am a prisoner here until Dec. 15 but shall go over then and see you before you go to America.

Yours ever
W. B. Yeats.

We very nearly wired to you to come over and play ' first musician.' Lady Gregory went so far as to put it to Fay—but our players woke up then. I don't think you would have liked to come but we would have been very urgent.

Nassau Hotel,
Sth. Frederick St,
Dublin, 6th Oct 1905.

My dear Florence Emery

I am dictating this because I have had an influenza cold for the last week and anything of that kind always affects my eyes and makes writing a much greater labour. I imagine I shall be over in London in a week or so but cannot say for certain. I have been kept all this while and am still kept by the affairs of the Theatre Society. We are turning it into a private Limited Liability Co. in order to get control into a few hands. If all goes well Lady Gregory, Synge and myself will be the Directors in a few days and will appoint Committees and have more votes between us than all the other shareholders. I have foreseen that something of this kind was inevitable from the first, but it has come rather sooner than I hoped for. I am pretty confident that we have the majority of the members with us in the change. It has been a very slow business winning their confidence, but I think we have it now. We have all the really competent people with us certainly. Hitherto the democratic arrangements have made it impossible to look ahead and settle dates and all that kind of thing. There were always too many people to consult. We started on our Autumn Session last Monday and are holding our audiences very well. This gets rid of my last anxiety for I have been sometimes afraid that our last years people came from curiosity and would fall off. I am now entirely certain that we will make a great Theatre and get an audience for it.

Did I tell you that the *Well of the Saints* has been accepted by a principal Theatre in Berlin ? It is a great triumph for us here as I foretold European Reputation for Synge at the Catholic College and have been mocked for the prophecy. All the incompetentness united in making little of that play and now its German acceptance comes just in time to prepare for the production of his new play an even wider business. He is a great man and I wish you could get a chance of playing him. I am still in the abyss over *Shadowy Waters*, it is not yet finished and my perplexity is as nothing to Fays over that shining harp. He and the stage carpenter are at this moment working away boring holes in the half of an old wooden bicycle wheel which is to play a mysterious part in the instrument. There are to be wonderful effects prepared for months beforehand, burning jewels on the harp and twinkling stars in the sky, but I imagine that both stars and jewels will slowly dwindle and fade as the night of performance gets near. Fay has just given me a good deal of pleasure by telling me that the players discussed last night in the Green Room whose plays drew the best and decided that mine did. I should not begrudge it to anyone if his plays drew more than mine, but it gives one more than a personal pleasure to find that anything so difficult as poetry can, under modern conditions, even hold its own against comedy in prose. Of course a good deal of this popularity comes from the fact that my name is better known than that of the others, but it does mean that I have a small genuine following as a dramatist. I think myself that in the long run Boyle and Lady Gregory will be our most popular playwrites. Her new play *The White Cockade* is a beautiful, laughing, joyful extravagant and yet altogether true phantasy. I have noticed, by the way, that the writers of this country who come from the mass of the people,—or no, I should say who come from Catholic Ireland, have more reason than fantasy. It is the other way with those who come from the leisured classes. They stand above their subject and play with it, and their writing is, as it were, a victory as well as a creation. The others—Colum and Edward Martyn for instance, are dominated by their subject, with the result that their work as a whole lacks beauty of shape the organic quality. They are never really gay though they can sometimes write about people who are. I wonder if this is true everywhere of the man of the people as contrasted with the man of traditional leisure. Of course Edward Martyn, on the father's side is one of the oldest families in Ireland, but he always seems to have more of his mother's temper, and besides he has taken the habit of his mind from the mass of the people. But philosophic generalisations are bad things

51

to set out on at five minutes to six with the type writing office about to close.

Write to me, but I daresay I shall write again in a day or two for I am not quite certain that a typewritten letter is a letter at all.

Yours ever
W. B. Yeats.

Nassau Hotel
South Frederick St
Dublin.

This damned beautiful weather is keeping our audience very thin—however we have enough money now to pay half a dozen of our people who are to go on tour. I sent you the play-book. I could not send it əs soon as said for somebody stole out of the Green Room the copy I bought for the purpose. General Meeting has been put off till Sunday. I shall therefore start home on Monday morning in time for my usual ' Monday.' You might come and dine that day if you have nothing else to do and keep Tuesday evening free for me. You can dine with me after the rehearsal. I may have nobody on Monday but most likely somebody will turn up. I was very glad to get your letter—a dip into the river of life changes even an old handwriting and gives it a new and meaning force.

I have not a moment to write in. I am expecting an unknown caller who was described to me by the hotel messenger boy as ' a gentleman with a shaking mouth ' called by name something like Holmes ! Examination of the boy reduced a ' shaking mouth ' to a stutter. I met Roberts a while ago—he had been to an Irish printers to arrange for the new publishing houses' first book. He said ' How much for a novel of 80,000 words ? ' The printers said ' Are they long words or short ? ' The path of the patriot is—well it is described by a popular phrase that has become common since my play, ' The Thorny path of Kathleen-ni-Houlihan.' *The Hour Glass* is beautiful now—Miss Walker a delight and Fay as Wise Man very varied and powerful.

The caller has come so—

Yours ever,
W. B. Yeats.

Nassau Hotel
South Frederick St.
Dublin.

My dear Florence Emery : thank you for your hint about the theatre. I will never mention it again. There is by the way a pretty scandal about—but I forgot I am not to speak of it. I want to see *Lady Inger** at (the) Stage Society but though I should see it at every cost I have not enough resolution to go over as I must return at once. If you can give me Tuesday morning afternoon or evening, or at worst Wednesday morning or afternoon or both I will come over on Monday see the play and return after having had a little of your company. I have to be here for a week or so after that as—but I forgot I have sworn. I have written to the Leeds man (from whom I heard) again asking for a date for us both in March and to know how much we can expect. I shall also write to Edinburgh where I go for two more lectures in March—or rather one there one at St. Andrews—and see if you can come. I want to see you very much now and it will always be a great pleasure to be with you.

* Produced January the 28th and 29th, 1906.

I have such a fine book to show you. Lord Lovelace's privately printed book about Byron and Mrs. Leigh, his half sister* A very vivid powerful book and not to be bought. I have been sent a copy and will bring it over. You cannot think what a pleasure it is to be fond of somebody to whom I can talk—as a rule any sort of affection annihilates conversation, strikes one with a silence like that of Adam before he had named the beasts. To be moved and talkative, unrestrained, one's own self, and to be this not because one has created some absurd delusion that it all is wisdom, as Adam may have in the beast's head, but not in Eve, but because one has found an equal, this is the best of life. All this means that I am looking forward to seeing you—that my spirits rise at the thought of it.

Synge—but I forget he is a part of what I have sworn off—well I cannot help it. His play was done in Germany in association with a play in one act by Wilde called I think *Florentine Nights*. I don't think it has been even published in England. Why not get it and play it at your new theatre.

Do help me to get over to the play. I won't go if you are not kind.

Yours ever
W. B. Yeats.

Coole Park
Gort
Co. Galway.
Tuesday.

My dear Florence Emery : I have sent *Ideas of Good and Evil* to Mrs. King, and I hope I shall be forgiven,

*"Astarte."

by you too, my too great preoccupation with your self. Mrs. Patrick Campbell, on whose tail I have not succeeded in dropping salt, should receive a copy of the new *Shadowy Waters* with a devout letter, but not yet. I myself—though I am still at Nassau Hotel—leave for Cork today to spend a couple of weeks of most unwilling industry—so great is your power. I think you may take the Leeds lecture as settled—but I have had to delay about Edinburgh until I get some other dates right. We shall have to make our own way in lecturing—one lecture will lead to another—we have not the advantage of the sort of popular subject which advertises a lecture by itself. Our reputations are too esoteric for the general public outside certain university towns. We shall make our way by our faculty, not by our subjects, in fame. This was what happened in my own case—I was refused by the agencies and then made hundreds of pounds. The second week in April would suit me for Oxford or Cambridge lecture.

I have been speaking here lately. I at least find that I can move people by power not merely—as the phrase is—by ' charm ' or ' speaking beautifully '—a thing I always resented. I feel this change in all my work and that it has brought a change into the personal relations of life—even things seemingly beyond control answer strangely to what is within. I once cared only for images about whose necks I could cast various ' chains of office ' as it were. They were so many aldermen of the ideal, whom I wished to master the city of the soul. Now I do not want images at all, or chains of office being contented with the unruly soul. I think you have changed too—is it that those eastern meditations have fired you—made you free of all but the holy church— now alas steering its malignant way, I suppose, through

55

the Indian Ocean—a sort of diabolical Aengus carrying not a glass house for Etain—as did the Irish one—but a whole convent, alter lights, vegetarian kitchen and all.

I have myself by the by begun eastern meditations of your sort, but with the object of trying to lay hands upon some dynamic and substantialising force as distinguished from the eastern quiescent and supersentualizing state of the soul—a movement downwards upon life not upwards out of life.

Yours ever
W. B. Yeats.

at Coole Park,
Gort
Co. Galway.
Friday.

My dear Florence Emery : I enclose a letter from Leeds and have written to say that you will write direct about posters etc. Don't you think that we should get some more of those hand bills or circulars about the " chanting " printed ? I will now try and arrange for Liverpool and Edinburgh but had better wait till I get exact dates in Dublin when I go tomorrow. I have done magnificent work here. I have a sketch of a strange little play about the capture of a blind Unicorn, and I have written a coral ode about witches which contain these lines—suggested in some vague way by your letter, only suggested I mean an phantasmal exageration of some sentence.

> Or, they hurl a spell at him
> That he follow with desire
> Bodies that can never tire

Or grow kind, for they anoint
All their bodies joint by joint
With a miracle working juice,
That is made out of the grease
Of the ungoverned unicorn ;
But the man is thrice forlorn
Emptied, ruined, wracked and lost
That *they* follow, for at most
They will give him kiss for kiss
While they murmur " After this
Hatred may be sweet in the taste."
Those wild hands that have embraced
All his body can but shove
At the burning wheel of love
Till the side of hate comes up.

The hero had been praising an indomitable kind of
woman and the chorus sing of her evil shadow. The
Unicorn in the little play is a type of masterful and
beautiful life but I shall not trouble to make the meaning clear—a clear vivid story of a strange sort is enough.
The meaning may be different with everyone.

I shall get you to teach me meditation. My difficulty
is that I get partly hypnotized at once and that a sleepy
calm makes it very difficult to get the mood of fiery
understanding which must represent the spirit which is,
according to the old definition, ' that which moves itself.'
I have never got this mood except in absolute trance at
night.

Yours always, shall I say affectionately or would that
arouse too much scorn.

W. B. Yeats.

I shall be back in London next week.

(Typed)

My dear Florence Farr, I think Bullen is going to put
all the music with all my other appendixes at the end of
the volume of prose plays as he wants to enlarge that
volume. I came up to Dublin last Thursday. We produced a play called the *Country Dressmaker*, a rough but
amusing piece of work which is showing signs of being
popular. I have got to a typewriter as you see and feel
I can tell the news at last. I have got so out of the habit
of writing letters with my fingers that even apart from
my sight I make them very short. I cannot recollect
whether I told you or not about Allen Bennett.* The
day I left London I was at the dentists' and he began
telling me about a friend of his, a man of science, who
was interested in Budhism. He had gone out to Burma
and there he met an Englishman who was a Buddhist
monk. This Englishman had converted him and now he
and the monk were members of a Buddhist missionary
Society. The Englishman was Allen Bennett. He showed
me a photographic group of the Committee of the Society
with Bennett in the middle, evidently the most important
person. He also told me that Bennett was now working
on experimental science. The friend and a native Bur-
mese widow and a third person paying the expenses. If
any profit resulted from Bennett's researches the bulk of
the profit is to go to the Missionary Society, but a certain
percentage to those who have supplied the capital. The
researches are concerned with N Rays. Bennett goes out
every morning with his begging bowl as a monk, but

* Allen Bennett, author of " The Wisdom of the Aryas," died in
1923.

always gives the contents of his bowl to some less well-provided for brother. His own meals are sent in every day to the workshop. I think I told you something of all this but not the details. I don't know when I shall be able to get over. I am desperately hard up owing to the difficulty of getting A. P. Watt and my publisher to meet. They have been playing some sort of a fantastic game for months. I got them together with much urgency last week with the only result that Bullen took offence because it was Watt junior who received him, and so went back to Stratford. In any case a man with Saturn entering his second house by transit has to look out for bad times. Astrology grows more and more wonderful every day. I have some astonishing irrefutable things to show you. I imagine that the stars are beginning to tell on Miss Horniman as since her first elated letter written the day after the start at Manchester I have not heard a word of how they are doing, though she has written about something else. I put the date of some great disturbance concerning her to April, May or June. I am trying to work at primary directions, but my head reels with all the queer, mathematical terms. I am hoping to find in the aspects a basis of evocation, which is really what interests me.

Did you see Bernard Shaw's letter in the " Times " a couple of days ago—logical, audacious and convincing, a really wonderful letter, at once violent and persuasive. He knew his opponent's case as well as his own, and that is just what men of his kind usually do not know. I saw *Caesar and Cleopatra* with Forbes Robertson in it twice this week and have been really delighted and what I never thought (to) be with work by him, moved. There is vulgarity, plenty of it, but such gay heroic delight in the serviceable mass. Ah if he had but style, and distinction and was not such a barbarian of the barricades. I am quite convinced by the by that the whole play is a half of you in your Egyptian period, and that you were the Cleopatra who offered that libation of wine to the table rapping sphinx.

Yours ever,

W. B. Yeats.

Coole Park,

Gort,

Co. Galway.

My dear Florence Emery: Here is the music—your old *Shadowy Waters* among the rest. I don't know if you have a version of the State Version (but you might leave that over for a little as I am hoping for copies of the American edition which contains it.) Keep the music safe for me. I don't find here that music you did for the womans song in *On Bailes Strand* and I must write again for it.

Miss Horniman is starting in Manchester on I think September 25 with that play of cockney life by Mac Evoy the Stage Society brought out a while back. I don't know what else she has but she claims to have lots of plays—they must be pretty bad if she has. I hear that Shaw advised Payne* to have nothing to do with her as she fights with everybody but Payne thinks he can manage. Lady Gregory says that Miss Horniman is like a shilling in a tub of electrified water—everybody tries to get the shilling out. Lady Gregory is now quite definitely added to Miss Hornimans list of truly wicked

* Mr. Shaw suggests that this reference is to Iden Payne.

people. I am looking forward to the moment when Manchester will begin to add our names. The strange thing is that any old hatred years after you think it dead will suddenly awake. They are like the stops of an organ.

I am reading Norths Plutarch and I find a beautiful thing. Alcebiades refused to learn the flute because he thought it ill became a gentleman to put his cheeks out of shape or to make music he could not speak to. He had so much influence that ever after the flute was despised. This might help you with your lectures—you will find it in the account of Alcebiades. Alcebiades said the flute should be left to Thebans that did not know how to speak. He also claimed that the patrons (of) Athens, Pallas and Apollo, objected to the flute and that Apollo skinned a man for playing on it.

Yours ever,
W. B. Yeats.

Coole Park
Gort
Co. Galway.

My dear Florence Emery : Agustus John has just left and I have time for letters. He has done numberless portraits of me to work up into an etching—all powerful ugly gypsey things. He behaved very well here, did the most wonderful acrobatic things on the floor and climbed to the top of the highest tree in the garden and did not talk much about his two wives and his seven children. Lady Gregory was always afraid some caller would say ' How many children ' ' Seven ' ' You must have married very young ' ' About four years ' ' Twins I suppose '

' Oh no but— ' and then all out. He wore hair down to his shoulders and an early victorian coat with a green velvet collar. Robert* watched him with ever visible admiration and dicipleship. To day Miss Horniman opens her Manchester theatre and for the next few months lives under the following secondary directions (nearly all from fifth house—house of theatres)

☽ ☍ ♃ R sep (arating)	Sept and Oct
☽ □ ☽ R	about Oct and Nov
☽ ☍ ♀ R ·	about Jan
☽ □ ☉ P	about March
☽ ☌ ♂ R	about July
☽ ☍ ♄ R	Nov and Dec

If this (and the transits are nearly as spirited) does not make hay with her Manchester theatre, Ananias was an astrologer and a planet and a star.

Many thanks about the music. The first five volumes are to come out almost at once. I think Miss Lyster† wrote as she did about Sidgewick because he and Bullen are I think on slightly strained relations. I have just glanced at your horoscope (but will work it out carefully). I note that ☽ is going to ☍ ♅, △ ☿ R, △ ♃ P, which should give you success in America (♃ ☌ ☿).

Yours ever
W. B. Yeats.

---

* Robert Gregory.

† Miss Lyster was a niece of A. H. Bullen who published Yeats' " Collected Works."

My dear Florence Emery : neither Lady Gregory nor
I would object to your playing *Shadow of the Glen* in the
small hall you speak of in your letter but I am afraid
you must do nothing for the present. Synge is very ill
in hospital and cannot be asked about any matter of
business. He is perhaps dying—nothing is known with
any certainty as the doctor don't know the nature of the
growth or whether it is the coming again of that growth
that has made him ill. He was very weak and pale when
I saw him a week ago. He is not allowed to see any one
except Molly Allgood who sees him for a few minutes
every second day. I cannot see him now for he finds
any conversation about literature too exciting. His
vitality is so low that he cannot read anything but the
lightest literature and does not leave his bed.

I find in Patmores book of Odes an appendex in which
he states our theory of music and speech very clearly.
In the 3.6 edition (*Poetical Works* Vol II) you will find
a long passage starting on page 232 which will interest
you and at any rate give you the support of a great
authority. I am grateful for your dedication and expect
to find your book very valuable.

I came down here for a few days to write in peace, but
not at *Player Queen*. My breakdown has left me with so
much to do I am afraid I must put *Player Queen* off for
a time as to do work of this kind amid all these distractions is a great strain and I don't do it well. If I can
get all the fundamental thinking through before the
summer I can finish the verse here in summer. Meanwhile I must do work that will bring in a little money

K

for Mrs. Campbell has sent me no agreement and when *Player Queen* is finished I may get nothing. She was to have paid me something on finishing the M.SS. I have a large MS book in which I write stray notes on all kind of things. These will make up into essays. They will amuse you very much. They are quite frank and the part that cannot be printed while I am alive is the amusing part.

I go to Dublin on Friday, I may be in London for a few days the first week in April.

Yours ever
W. B. Yeats.

at Coole Park,
Gort
Co. Galway.

My dear Florence Emery : the result of your sending me those lines—alas—to put into charitable English is that I have never written to you. I have been ashamed to write and not send them and I have always had so much to do. I am in the worst stage of a new play— the dreadful opening work on the scenario—working badly because one hates the work. I shall have no leisure or pleasure in life until I begin the verse writing and when this comes life will be worth having again and I shall have moments for my friends. As it is I sit down at 11, idle for an hour perhaps and then work an hour and then half idle half work and so till tea and five o'clock comes round and my heart and my conscience both are aching. I was only one day in London on my way from Paris driven on by this work. Have you seen Mrs. Campbell ? Do you know what she plans to do ?

Is she really going to come here. I have put Deidre into rehearsal but I have never really believed she would play in it.

I have a fine tale of Althea Gyles. She brought a prosperous love-affair to an end by reading Browning to the poor man in the middle of the night. She collects the necessities of life from her friends and spends her own money on flowers.

I should think you will have your copy of the collected edition in about three weeks. I have written to them to put in the Agustus John after all.

My father is still in America. He gave orders that no windows were ever to be opened. A window was opened by the house maid, and a Musketo got in. His letters are full of the Musketo. He makes after dinner speeches and is evidently in great content.

I have heard nothing of you this long time so please write and tell me about Mrs. Campbell. I know she has been thinking of altering her dates.

Yours ever
W. B. Yeats.

18, Woburn Buildings,
Euston Road,
London.
April 21. 1908

My dear Florence Emery : I sent The M(int ?). I called at the office and it was shut up for the holidays (and) bribed a sort of office boy to get a copy sent to you. I then got a copy myself after going to four book stalls which had none left.

I am just off to Stratford-on-Avon where Sarah All-good plays Issabella—we have lent her to Poel—in *Measure for Measure*. She has made a great success in the part at Manchester. Mrs. Campbell has announced that she will do Miss Tobins *Phedra* in London. You must be got to play in that. The second heroine is a very fine part and would suit you in some ways well.

When do you return. There is a slight chance of my going to Paris at once for a week though I don't think it likely. I wonder will you be there on your way. Let me know your plans at any rate. London is unendurable when you are not in it. I have no real friends—I have been too long away—and wander about without a soul to whom I can talk as if to myself. I go to bad plays or blind myself with reading by candle light out of boredom.

Here is Condres* account given to Sargent of how he came to enjoy music first. " I never understood it until one day I thought it was like pink satin. I was going home one night in Paris. There was a decadent poet with me. He had a revolver. He fired it through key-holes. He shot off several bolts. Then a policeman took him away. His mistress was with us and I said ' Come with me and sleep on the sofa.' She slept on the sofa and I went to my room. In the middle of the night I heard a sound of broken glass. She had climbed through the sky light and was calling to the police to protect her from me. A friend said nobody can help you now but the archbishop of Paris and when he came next day to the prison the archbishop was dressed in pink satin. That is how I came to understand music."

Yours ever

W. B. Yeats.

* Perhaps Charles Conder, the fan-painter.

18, Woburn Buildings,
Upper Woburn Place, W. C.
June 27

Dear Mrs. Emery : I do not think I can get to you this afternoon. The usual theatre distractions draw me to Lindsay House at 5 and at 7.30 I dine with Rothenstein to meet Tagore the Hindu poet. I am engaged to morrow afternoon (Friday). Can I come Saturday at 5.30 or six. We could dine somewhere and go on to the theatre where there will be a new play by Boyle.

I had a sceance last night with Mrs Thompson, Myers Medium, very interesting though nothing exactly evidential. The control Nelly came—it was curious to watch the sudden change in the midst of a lively conversation. Nelly spoke of being in the Medium's stomach (her mother's stomach she said) and complained that there was still some Medium left in the head. She distinguished between what she got from spirits and what she saw in our stomachs. I was introduced as Mr. Smith. Nelly said my stomach was hard to read (her phrase was not clear or clean) and that I should wear a black beard and a white robe and be a Yogi priest and that she was uncomfortable because my hypnotism " screwed out Mother's stomach " instead of Mothers " screwing out " mine as it should be. She told me that in her own home she understood things, that there she got into a state which she called ' crysalis,' a state it seems of partial unconsciousness though she felt people in it but they had no ' bodies ' or ' feet or boots ' and then she got at mother's stomach and could see nothing but what mother saw, and felt like ' a wet chicken.' If she could only come straight without being a crysalis she could tell a lot.

Yours

W. B. Yeats.